THE HOLY SPIRIT

Study Guide

KENNETH COPELAND

THE HOLY SPIRIT

Study Guide

KENNETH COPELAND

KENNETH
COPELAND
PUBLICATIONS

The Holy Spirit

ISBN-10 1-57562-696-9   30-0726
ISBN-13 978-1-57562-696-3

23 22 21 20 19 18   14 13 12 11 10 9

Kenneth Copeland Publications
Fort Worth, TX 76192-0001

For more information about Kenneth Copeland Ministries, visit kcm.org or call 1-800-600-7395 (U.S. only) or +1-817-852-6000.

1

"But ye shall
receive power, after that
the Holy Ghost is
come upon you."

Acts 1:8

The Holy Spirit is the muscle or

the power of God. That power is

available to every believer.

CD ONE

Reality of the Holy Spirit I

"*N*ow unto him that is
able to do exceeding abundantly
above all that we ask or think, *according
to the power that worketh in us....*"
Ephesians 3:20

As Believers, We Receive Power When the Holy Spirit Comes to Live in Us

FOCUS: "Finally, my brethren, be strong in the Lord, and in the power of his might" (Ephesians 6:10). With the indwelling Holy Spirit, we have the power of God Himself within us.

The Bible introduces us to the Holy Spirit at Creation. Genesis 1:1-3 says, "In the beginning God created the heaven and the earth.... And the spirit of God moved upon the face of the waters. And God said, Let there be light: and there was light." At the very first mention of the Holy Spirit, He's moving. And the first creative act we see in the Bible is at the hands of the Holy Spirit.

> *With the indwelling Holy Spirit, we have the power of God Himself within us.*

The Holy Spirit is the muscle or the power of God. The Greek word for this type of power is translated *dynamo* or *dynamite*. It is self-energizing, explosive, moving. It is the same power spoken of in Acts 1:8: "But ye shall receive power, after that the Holy Ghost is come upon you..." and in Ephesians 3:20: "Now unto him that is able to do exceeding abundantly above all that we ask or think, according to the power that worketh in us."

There is another word translated *power* that means "authority." In Colossians 1:12-13, the word *power* is not speaking of the dynamo kind of power of the Holy Spirit, but of the authority given to believers: "Giving thanks unto the Father...who hath delivered us from the power of darkness, and hath translated us into the kingdom of his dear Son." We have authority over the enemy (see Luke 10:19).

But we also need the dynamo power of the Holy Spirit. Ephesians 6:10 says, "Finally, my brethren, be strong in the Lord, and in the power of his might."

Jesus received that power when the Holy Spirit came on Him. Acts 10:38 says, "How God anointed Jesus of Nazareth with the Holy Ghost and with power: who went about doing good, and healing all that were oppressed of the devil; for God was with him."

That same power is available to you through the indwelling Holy Spirit. But the Holy Spirit only comes in when He is invited by faith. He won't force Himself on you. You must ask in faith and believe you receive (Luke 11:13).

When you receive the Holy Spirit, when He comes in and personally dwells inside you, it is the joining of two persons—you and the Holy Spirit. There is an intermingling that takes place. He comes to live in your re-created human spirit to be your intercessor, your standby, your comforter, your teacher, your guide. And He has put in you, by His presence, all the power He possesses.

First John 4:4 says, "Ye are of God, little children, and have overcome them: because greater is he that is in you, than he that is in the world." Not only have we overcome the enemy and been given authority over him, but we can successfully stand against him because *the Greater One lives in us.*

The only thing keeping that power bound is the words we speak. Ephesians 4:29-30 says, "Let no corrupt communication proceed out of your mouth.... And grieve not the holy Spirit of God...." Guard your mouth. Don't speak words that offend the Holy Spirit, like words of unforgiveness, disharmony or unbelief. God can't afford to back that corrupt communication with His power. Instead, speak based on the Word of God. God can only turn up the power as He trusts the words that come out our mouths.

Realize who is inside you. He is the One who measured and calculated from a single drop of water in His hand, every moisture change and exchange

> *Realize who you have on the inside of you.*

that would ever take place in this universe. He is the One who comprehended the dust of the earth and figured out how to compensate for all the times the earth would shift, be rearranged and changed physically but still rotate through space on its axis, undisturbed (Isaiah 40:12-13).

> The mighty Spirit of God is living in you, so become God-inside-minded. Second Corinthians 6:16 says, "For ye are the temple of the living God; as God hath said, I will dwell in them, and walk in them; and I will be their God, and they shall be my people."

What does it mean for Him to be God to us? Philippians 4:19 says, "But my God shall supply all your need according to his riches in glory by Christ Jesus." In this verse, the word *God* is the Hebrew, *El Shaddai,* "The Breasty One—Nurse, Mother, Father, Supplier, Brother, Sister, Provider"—anything and everything

> **Become God-inside-minded.**

we need. He is supreme. He is all-powerful. He is almighty. There is none greater.

He is not off in space somewhere, but living and working in us because we are new creations in Him. He is as close as our very breath. Philippians 2:13 says, "For it is God Who is all the while effectually at work in you [energizing and creating in you the

power and desire], both to will and to work for His good pleasure..."
(The Amplified Bible).

Now Begin Enjoying It

As believers, our goal should be to walk in the fullness of the power of God. Yet, we have only scratched the surface of what the Spirit of God is capable of doing inside us. You see, it is up to us how much we will walk in the power of God. He operates according to our faith in the Word. As we totally commit to His Word and allow Him to lead us by it, we will know the working of His power.

CD 1 Outlined

I. The Holy Spirit is the power of God, the muscle of God
    A. Dynamo or dynamite power—self-energizing, moving, explosive, energy-producing power
    B. We first see Him working in Creation (Genesis 1:1-3)

II. The Holy Spirit is a Person who dwells inside the new creation
    A. You are the temple of the Living God (2 Corinthians 6:16)
    B. He intermingles and becomes one with you by faith invitation (Luke 11:13)

III. When you receive the Holy Spirit, His power is in you (Acts 1:8; Ephesians 3:20)
    A. God can turn up the power as we order our words
    B. Jesus walked in the fullness of the power of God (Acts 10:38)

IV. Realize who you have living inside you
    A. He is the Creator of the universe
    B. Become God-inside-minded

V. He dwells in us and is God to us
    A. Philippians 4:19 defines how He is God to us—He supplies all our needs
    B. "He is *El Shaddai*—The Breasty One—anything and everything we need
    C. He is supreme; there is none greater or higher
    D. He is as close as our breath

Study Questions

(1) Define *dynamo* power. _____
_____
_____
_____
_____

(2) Explain the difference between the power of the Holy Spirit and your authority as a believer. _____
_____
_____
_____

(3) What hinders the Holy Spirit from turning up the power in the believer? _____
_____
_____
_____
_____

(4) What determines His capabilities in you?_____
_____
_____
_____
_____

(5) What does it mean for God to be a God to you? _____
_____
_____
_____

Study Notes

_____

_____

_____

_____

_____

_____

_____

_____

_____

_____

_____

_____

_____

_____

_____

_____

_____

_____

_____

_____

_____

_____

_____

*"Howbeit when he, the Spirit of truth, is come,
he will guide you into all truth...."*
John 16:13

2

"And I will pray the Father, and he shall give you another Comforter, that he may abide with you for ever; even the Spirit of truth; whom the world cannot receive, because it seeth him not, neither knoweth him: but ye know him; for he dwelleth with you, and shall be in you."

John 14:16-17

Jesus prayed for the Holy Spirit to come

and dwell in the believer.

CD TWO
Reality of the Holy Spirit II

"Nevertheless I tell you the truth;
It is expedient for you that I go away:
for if I go not away, the Comforter
will not come unto you; but if I depart,
I will send him unto you."

John 16:7

Jesus Sent the Holy Spirit to Dwell in Believers, to Teach and Empower Them

FOCUS: "I have yet many things to say unto you, but ye cannot bear them now. Howbeit when he, the Spirit of truth, is come, he will guide you into all truth..." (John 16:12-13).

Jesus, talking to the disciples at the close of His ministry on earth, said it was more profitable for Him to go away so that the Comforter (Holy Spirit) could come (John 16:7). That was a hard saying for them to understand. For three years they had witnessed the miracles Jesus had done. He had met their every need with the faith and power of God. They must have wondered how it could possibly be better for Him to go away.

The disciples didn't know it then, but the coming of the Holy Spirit to indwell them would make it possible for them to walk in the same power in which Jesus walked.

Under the old covenant, the dwelling place of the Holy Spirit was in the holy of holies. When He came upon men, great manifestations of God's power took place.

At the time of Jesus' crucifixion, the Holy Spirit tore the 4-inch-thick curtain of the temple from the top to the bottom and moved out of that earth-made holy of holies. He went into hell itself and raised Jesus from the dead.

After that, the Holy Spirit began His ministry in the earth in the hearts of men. He has never dwelt in a man-made tabernacle again. The same power that raised Jesus from the dead dwells in you as a new creation in Christ. You are now the temple of the Holy Spirit (1 Corinthians 6:19).

Second Corinthians 6:16 says, "Ye are the temple of the living God; as God hath said, I will dwell in them, and walk in them...."

God is not some strange, huge being. According to Isaiah 40:12, He measured out heaven with the span of His hand. A span is the distance between the tip of the little finger and the end of the thumb. The Hebrew Bible says He measured heaven with a 9-inch span. That's about the size of a man's hand. You see, we are more in His image than we have ever really conceived.

We are living stones of which the house of God is being built. That house is a giant in the world—a mobile temple not made with hands—the Body of Christ. The Holy Spirit is living in each of us individually, but also working in us collectively. We are one with Him.

The Holy Spirit is the Teacher of the Church. Jesus said in John 14:26, "But the Comforter, which is the Holy Ghost, whom the Father will send in my name, he shall teach you all things, and bring all things to your remembrance, whatsoever I have said unto you."

> *The Holy Spirit is the Teacher of the Church.*

Under the old covenant, men had to have a special dispensation of God or else be called as a prophet, king, Levite or priest to receive revelation knowledge from the Holy Spirit. But today every born-again believer has a right to know the deep things of God. Jesus said, "All things that the Father hath are mine: therefore said I, that he [the Holy Spirit] shall take of mine, and shall show it unto you" (John 16:15). First Corinthians 2:7-12 says this:

> But we speak the wisdom of God in a mystery, even the hidden wisdom, which God ordained before the world unto our glory: which none of the princes of this world knew: for had they known it, they would not have crucified the Lord of glory. But as it is written, Eye hath not seen, nor ear heard, neither have entered into the heart of man, the things which God hath prepared for them that love him. But God hath revealed them unto

us by his Spirit: for the Spirit searcheth all things, yea, the deep things of God. For what man knoweth the things of a man, save the spirit of man which is in him? even so the things of God knoweth no man, but the Spirit of God. Now we have received, not the spirit of the world, but the spirit which is of God; that we might know the things that are freely given to us of God.

No one knows what is in the heart of a man except the spirit of a man. Even so, the Holy Spirit knows God. When He comes to dwell in our spirits, we can know the things of God because He will reveal them to us.

We have the mind of Christ (1 Corinthians 2:16). As we meditate in the Word and allow the Holy Spirit to reveal that Word to us, His thoughts become our thoughts.

The mystery of God—the entire plan of redemption—is hidden from the world, but it has been revealed to the Church. "That their hearts might be comforted, being knit together in love, and unto all riches of the full assurance of understanding, to the acknowledgement of the mystery of God, and of the Father, and of Christ; in whom are hid all the treasures of wisdom and knowledge" (Colossians 2:2-3). All treasures are *in* Christ. We are *in* Christ and He is *in* us. All the wisdom and knowledge God possesses is residing inside us, just waiting for the Holy Spirit to reveal it to us.

> *Every believer has a right to know the deep things of God.*

Jesus was right when He said it was more profitable that He go away so He could send the Comforter. That Greater One is living in you right now. The Creator of the universe who fashioned and computed all of this in the palm of His hand has come to dwell in you and walk in you.

Now Begin Enjoying It

Begin to pray in the spirit and let the Holy Spirit instruct you. He's ready to reveal the mysteries and the wisdom of God. He's ready to empower you.

ℭ𝒟 2 𝒪𝓊𝓉𝓁𝒾𝓃𝑒𝒹

I. It was profitable for Jesus to go away so the Comforter could come and believers could walk as Jesus walked (John 16:7)

II. Under the old covenant, the holy of holies was the earthly dwelling place of the Holy Spirit
   A. Now He inhabits a new temple—the spirits of men (1 Corinthians 6:19)
   B. As He continues to intermingle with believers, the house of God becomes a giant mobile temple

III. Under the old covenant, a special dispensation or calling was needed to receive revelation

IV. Under the new covenant, every believer can receive revelation because the Holy Spirit lives inside us
   A. The Holy Spirit is the Teacher of the Church
   B. The mystery of God—the entire plan of redemption—is revealed through godly wisdom and understanding by the Holy Spirit

V. We are *in* Christ and He is *in* us
   A. All treasures are in Christ
   B. All the wisdom and knowledge God possesses is residing inside the believer
   C. Become God-inside-minded

$Study$ $Questions$

(1) Why would the Holy Spirit's coming be profitable to man?_____

_____

_____

_____

(2) Under the new covenant, where is the dwelling place of the Holy Spirit?_____

_____

_____

(3) Explain how the house of God becomes a giant mobile temple in the earth. _____

_____

_____

_____

(4) Why do we have the mind of Christ? _____

_____

_____

_____

(5) What has been revealed to the Church that has been hidden from the world? _____

_____

_____

_____

Study Notes

"Ye are the temple of the living God; as God hath said,
I will dwell in them, and walk in them; and I will
be their God, and they shall be my people."
2 Corinthians 6:16

3

"For as many are led by the Spirit of God, they are the sons of God."

Romans 8:14

"My sheep hear my voice, and I know them, and they follow me."

John 10:27

Learn to recognize and follow the inward

voice. Let the Holy Spirit lead you.

CD THREE
Reality of the Holy Spirit III

"Howbeit when he, the Spirit of
truth, is come, he will guide you into
all truth: for he shall not speak of
himself; but whatsoever he shall
hear, that shall he speak...."
John 16:13

*I*f you're a believer, you have the
ability and right to be led by the Holy
Spirit. But it's up to you to learn how
to do that and make it a priority in
your life.

The Holy Spirit Is Still Available to Us Today and Extremely Profitable for Us to Receive

FOCUS: "For as many as are led by the Spirit of God, they are the sons of God" (Romans 8:14).

Jesus told His disciples in John 16:12-13, "I have yet many things to say unto you, but ye cannot bear them now. Howbeit when he, the Spirit of truth, is come, he will guide you into all truth…." Until man receives the Holy Spirit, he can't understand the deep things of God and His Word. He needs the Holy Spirit to lead and guide him.

How do we receive and utilize this invaluable gift that Jesus has sent us? Luke 11 provides some insight: "If a son shall ask bread of any of you that is a father, will he give him a stone? or if he ask a fish, will he for a fish give him a serpent? or if he shall ask an egg, will he offer him a scorpion? If ye then, being evil, know how to give good gifts unto your children: how much more shall your heavenly Father give the Holy Spirit to them that ask him?" (verses 11-13).

> *Being filled with the Holy Spirit does not mean you are led by the Spirit.*

Notice this says "If a *son* shall ask…." First, a person must make Jesus Christ the Lord of his life and be born of the Spirit of God. Then, he simply asks the Father in Jesus' Name. Those are the only requirements for being filled with the Holy Spirit. The only thing that can keep a born-again believer from receiving the Baptism in the Holy Spirit is not asking.

However, being filled with the Holy Spirit does not necessarily mean you are always being *led* by the Spirit. To be led by Him, you must be attentive and obedient to His voice.

You have the capability to hear Him. Jesus said His sheep hear His voice (John 10:27). And Romans 8:14 says, "For as many as are led by the Spirit of God, they are the sons of God." If you are a believer, He is speaking to you all the time. The important thing to learn is how to consistently listen.

First, learn to recognize His voice. When God speaks, He always speaks the same as His Word. The Bible says all the promises of God in Him are "yes and amen!" (2 Corinthians 1:20). God says things like, "All things are possible to him that believeth" (Mark 9:23). He always speaks success, faith and encouragement.

God speaks to your spirit. The voice of your spirit is your conscience. Before you are saved, it is not in tune with the things of God. First Corinthians 2:14-16 says, "But the natural man receiveth not the things of the Spirit of God: for they are foolishness unto him: neither can he know them, because they are spiritually discerned. But he that is spiritual judgeth all things, yet he himself is judged of no man. For who hath known the mind of the Lord, that he may instruct him? But we have the mind of Christ."

After you are saved and the Holy Spirit comes to dwell inside you, you have the ability to recognize the voice of God as He speaks to your spirit. Your spirit is re-created and is in tune with the things of God.

With the Holy Spirit abiding in you, you can receive revelation knowledge and insight into the things of God. Colossians 1:9 says, "We...desire that ye might be filled with the knowledge of his will in all wisdom and spiritual understanding." The Greek text says, "…be filled with exact knowledge." That's what is also called "revelation knowledge." It is knowledge that is revealed by the Spirit of God to the spirit of man.

The reborn human spirit can be developed and it has a voice—the inward witness.

An underdeveloped inward witness of your spirit is what we sometimes refer to as a "hunch." In other words, "I just felt like I shouldn't go" or "I feel like that isn't what I should do." As you develop in following after that voice, you readily recognize and consistently follow that inward leading.

One way you develop your ability to follow the inward witness is by praying in the spirit. The Apostle Paul said, "For if I pray in an [unknown] tongue, my spirit [by the Holy Spirit within me] prays…" (1 Corinthians 14:14, *The Amplified Bible*).

When a believer is praying in the spirit, or praying in other tongues by the Holy Spirit, he is speaking to God and not to man (verse 2). He is being edified, or charged, with spiritual power, building himself up on his most holy faith (Jude 20).

This is where you grow and develop spiritually. The more you pray in the spirit, the more you recognize the inward voice. You are moved by and listen to what goes on in the world of the spirit. You are led by the Spirit.

Now Begin Enjoying It

Meditate in the Word of God, pray in the spirit, listen and give God an opportunity to speak. Stay there until your mind gets quiet and the peace of God rises from within you.

Then pray to interpret what you have been praying in the spirit (1 Corinthians 14:13). The Holy Spirit will begin to teach you and train you.

Be willing to learn, and do not be afraid to make mistakes. The biggest mistake is never attempting to hear from God at all. Remember this: If you are seeking Him, He's bigger than your mistakes.

CD 3 Outlined

I. The only thing that keeps a born-again believer from being filled with the Spirit is not asking the Father for Him

II. Being filled with the Holy Spirit does not mean you are led by the Spirit
   A. You must hear the voice of the Holy Spirit to be led by Him
   B. Believers are able to hear and be led by the Spirit (Romans 8:14; John 10:27)

III. The voice of your spirit is your conscience
   A. The natural man doesn't receive the things of God (1 Corinthians 2:14)
   B. The believer's re-created spirit is in tune with the things of God

IV. You can be filled with exact knowledge (Colossians 1:9)
   A. Exact knowledge is revelation knowledge from the Holy Spirit
   B. The Holy Spirit reveals truth (John 16:13)

V. Development of the inward witness is praying in tongues

VI. Praying in the spirit edifies and builds you up on your most holy faith (Jude 20)

VII. To hear the voice of your spirit, do these things:
   A. Meditate on the Word
   B. Pray in the spirit
   C. Listen to God speak

Study Questions

(1) What enables men to have the Word revealed to them?_____

_____

_____

_____

_____

(2) What keeps a born-again believer from being filled with the Spirit?

_____

_____

_____

_____

(3) What is the voice of your spirit? _____

_____

_____

_____

_____

(4) How do you develop the inward witness? _____

_____

_____

_____

_____

(5) How do you hear the voice of the Spirit?_____

_____

_____

_____

_____

Study Notes

_____

_____

_____

_____

_____

_____

_____

_____

_____

_____

_____

_____

_____

_____

_____

_____

_____

_____

_____

_____

_____

_____

*"But ye, beloved, building up yourselves on your most
holy faith, praying in the Holy Ghost."*
Jude 20

4

*"God is faithful, by whom
ye were called unto the
fellowship of his Son
Jesus Christ our Lord."*

1 Corinthians 1:9

You are called to fellowship with God…

through Jesus Christ.

CD FOUR
Fellowshiping With the Father

"Truly our fellowship
is with the Father, and
with his Son Jesus Christ."
1 John 1:3

God created you to fellowship
with Him. Take a step of faith and
reach out to Him. He's waiting to
hear from you.

Fellowship Was the Reason for the Creation of Mankind

FOCUS: "Draw near to God and He will draw near to you…" (James 4:8, *New King James Version*).

The believer is called by God into fellowship through the Lord Jesus Christ. This fellowship brings the believer into the presence of God and causes his joy to be full (see 1 John 1:3-4; Psalm 16:11). It also causes him to be filled with knowledge and enriched in every area of life (1 Corinthians 1:5).

God desired a being in His own class with whom He could fellowship. He could not fellowship with angels. They were not created in His class, and they are not born of God.

> *Fellowship was the reason for the creation of mankind.*

So God desired a family. When He created man, He created him in His image and likeness. He created man in His class so there could be relationship and fellowship. But when Adam fell, man's relationship with God was severed. That's why He had to send Jesus.

When you are born again, old things pass away and all things become new. The re-creation of your spirit makes you a child of God. You become a member of the family of God in Christ Jesus. Your relationship with God is restored through the lordship of Jesus.

But relationship without fellowship is like marriage without love. People in that situation are a family, but they do not have fellowship with one another because they have not taken the time to know one another. That is why it is so important when your relationship with God is restored through the new birth that you fellowship with Him on a consistent basis. Talk to Him. Spend time in the Word and pray in the spirit. Get to know Him. You will find that your relationship with God is deeply enriched by your fellowship with Him.

How does God fellowship? How do we get to know Him? Second Peter 1:3-4 says, "…through the knowledge of him…are given unto us exceeding great and precious promises: that by these ye might be partakers of the divine nature…." We partake of the divine nature of God through His promises. All the promises of God are in Him "yes and amen!" (2 Corinthians 1:20). When we receive His promises and activate them in faith, He will perform His Word on our behalf. But it all starts with fellowship.

When fellowship with God is broken, Satan will see to it that circumstances arise to try and convince you that God is the problem. God never is, nor will He ever be, the problem. He is the answer, whatever the need. Through fellowship with Him, you walk in the confidence that He is at work in your life.

Fellowship is the mother of faith.

Fellowship is the mother of faith. The more you talk and commune with God, the more you will trust Him. The more you fellowship with Him, the more you will know "He is *for* me, not against me." Your confidence to act on His Word in faith will grow, and you will realize that a very close relationship between you and the Father has developed.

.

Talk with God just because you love Him. Don't wait until you need something before you go to Him.

Hebrews 4:16 says we can come boldly to the throne of grace. But if you wait until you have a need and do not have constant daily fellowship with God, your relationship with Him will seem distant. It shouldn't be that way. He's a friend who sticks closer than a brother (Proverbs 18:24). James 4:8 says if you draw near to Him, He will draw near to you. In fact, if you're born again, He's right there, living inside you now.

Jesus said, "I in them, and thou [God] in me, that they may be made perfect in one; and that the world may know that thou hast sent me, and hast loved them, as thou hast loved me" (John 17:23). God loves you as much as He loves Jesus. He is ready to answer your prayers. Knowing He loves you gives you confidence to act on His Word.

Now Begin Enjoying It

When you keep God's Word and put it first place in your life, He manifests Himself to you and causes you to eat the good of the land (Isaiah 1:19). Jesus said, "If a man love me, he will keep my words: and my Father will love him, and we will come unto him, and make our abode with him" (John 14:23).

How does God feel about fellowship? Look at Revelation 3:20: "Behold, I stand at the door, and knock: if any man hear my voice, and open the door, I will come in to him, and will sup with him, and he with me." God is knocking at the door of your heart, desiring fellowship with you. Why not open the door and invite Him in?

CD 4 Outlined

I. The believer is called to fellowship with the Father through His Son Jesus Christ (1 John 1:3)
   A. Fellowship causes joy to be made full because there is joy in the presence of God (Psalm 16:11)
   B. Fellowship causes the believer to be filled with knowledge and enriched in every area of life (1 Corinthians 1:5)

II. God created man for fellowship, so man was created in God's class

III. Relationship made fellowship possible
   A. Relationship is sonship by new birth
   B. When you are born-again, you become a child of God

IV. Fellowship is how you get to know someone

V. Fellowship is the mother of faith
   A. Fellowship with God builds trust to act on His Word
   B. Through fellowship you learn that God is *for* you, not against you

VI. Commune with God because He is God and you love Him

VII. God loves you and wants to manifest Himself to you (John 17:23, John 14:23; Revelation 3:20)

Study Questions

(1) Why was man created in the image and likeness of God? _____

_____

_____

_____

_____

(2) What is your relationship with God?_____

_____

_____

_____

_____

(3) What made fellowship with God possible? _____

_____

_____

_____

_____

(4) How does God fellowship? _____

_____

_____

_____

_____

(5) Why is fellowship the mother of faith?_____

_____

_____

_____

Study Notes

_____

_____

_____

_____

_____

_____

_____

_____

_____

_____

_____

_____

_____

_____

_____

_____

_____

_____

_____

_____

_____

_____

"That in every thing ye are enriched by him,
in all utterance, and in all knowledge."

1 Corinthians 1:5

5

"Looking unto Jesus the author and finisher of our faith.... Consider him... lest ye be wearied and faint in your minds."

Hebrews 12:2-3

Don't waste time looking at your

problems. Look at Jesus.... Look at

the Word...and receive it by faith!

CD FIVE
Consider Jesus

*L*ook to the Word of God and all Jesus has done, and receive it by faith. Consider this: Jesus is bigger than all your problems!

The Just Shall Live by Faith

FOCUS: "So then faith cometh by hearing, and hearing by the word of God" (Romans 10:17).

When you were born again, you were dealt the measure of faith, which came to reside in your spirit. Jesus is the Author and Developer of that faith. He is the living Word of God (John 1:1).

> *Jesus is the Author and Developer of your faith.*

> Looking unto Jesus the author and fin- isher of our faith; who for the joy that was set before him endured the cross, despising the shame, and is set down at the right hand of the throne of God. For consider him that endured such contra- diction of sinners against himself, lest ye be wearied and faint in your minds (Hebrews 12:2-3).

It is your responsibility to look to Jesus. It is your responsibility, as a believer, to exercise your faith in the Word of God and walk in the results it produces. "Now faith is the substance of things hoped for, the evidence of things not seen" (Hebrews 11:1). The Word says, "The just shall live by faith" (Romans 1:17). As far as God is concerned, you should be living by the force of faith. To live otherwise is not liv- ing in the benefits He has provided for you. You don't have to wait until you get to heaven to receive those benefits. You can receive them now through faith in Jesus.

So consider Jesus, the Word, rather than your weakness. Become more aware of the Word of God that is true, than what you feel and see. Keep your circumstances out of your thinking, and think instead about what Jesus did for you at Calvary. The redemption and benefits

He provided belong to you *now* as a born-again believer. They are yours by faith. If you think about what you cannot do, you are preparing to fail. Instead consider Jesus. Consider the Word. Base your faith on the Word of God that never fails. You will see the results of that work in your life.

The Word says to consider Jesus and not be weary and faint in your mind. Do not relax and grow tired in your mind, but fight the good fight of faith. Renew your mind to the Word of God. As you meditate in the Word, it builds an inner image of success. You see yourself healed, prosperous, righteous and having peace of mind. No matter what anyone says or what circumstances may come your way, the Word remains true. Keep it first place and final authority, and you will see it come to pass.

For the Word to be final authority in your life, it means you must stand on it, regardless. You do not compromise for any reason. For the Word to be final authority, it means the Word controls your speech. Every time you hear someone say something, you think, *What does the Word say about that?* The Word is the guideline for everything you say and do. When the Word is final authority, you don't confer with flesh and blood.

> *For the Word to be final authority, it means you stand on the Word, regardless.*

Here is a three-step formula for success: Step one: Find out the will of God in the situation you are facing. Step two: When you are sure of the will of God, then no longer confer with flesh and blood. Step three: Get the job done at any cost, by faith.

The Word causes faith to be active. "So then faith cometh by hearing, and hearing by the word of God" (Romans 10:17). The Word of God is the will of God. In His desire for man to know Him, God put His inner thoughts, will and purpose into words. Then He sent the

Holy Spirit to reveal those truths to us. His words are life to us—the living Word of God.

> *When you look to the Word, you are looking to Jesus. Jesus and the Word are one, and they are in perfect agreement.*

Jesus said in John 15:7-8, "If ye abide in me, and my words abide in you, ye shall ask what ye will, and it shall be done unto you. Herein is my Father glorified, that ye bear much fruit...." Feeding the reborn human spirit with the Word of God eventually causes fruit to come forth. As you release your faith with your mouth based on what the Word says, the desired result will be produced.

Now Begin Enjoying It

No one can stop you from receiving when Jesus is your Lord and you act in faith. So consider Jesus in all you say and do. See the victory through the eye of faith and speak words of faith. You have inside you the same substance from which the whole universe was formed. You have the very power and provision of God at your disposal. Now that's something to consider!

CD 5 Outlined

I. You received the measure of faith when you were born again
  A. Jesus is the Author and Developer of your faith (Hebrews 12:2-3)
  B. God expects you to live by faith (Hebrews 11:1; Romans 1:17)

II. Consider Jesus, the Author and Finisher of your faith
  A. Do not consider your own weaknesses and failures
  B. Do not be weary and faint in your mind
    1. Fight the good fight of faith
    2. Renew your mind to the Word of God

III. Make the Word final authority
  A. Stand on the Word, regardless
  B. Order your conversation according to what the Word says

IV. Here are three steps to success
  A. Find out if it is God's will
  B. Once you know the will of God, no longer confer with flesh and blood
  C. Get the job done at any cost

V. The Word causes faith to be active
  A. The Word is God's thoughts, will and purpose put into written form
  B. God sent the Holy Spirit to reveal those truths to us in the Word
  C. Jesus and the Word are one and in agreement

Study Questions

(1) Why is it possible for the just to live by faith? _____

_____

_____

_____

_____

(2) What should we consider rather than our failures and weaknesses?

_____

_____

_____

_____

(3) How do you fight the good fight of faith? _____

_____

_____

_____

_____

(4) What builds an inner image of success? _____

_____

_____

_____

(5) What does it mean for the Word to be final authority?_____

_____

_____

_____

_____

Study Notes

"For therein is the righteousness of God revealed from faith
to faith: as it is written, The just shall live by faith."
Romans 1:17

6

"Out of the mouth of babes and sucklings hast thou ordained strength because of thine enemies, that thou mightest still the enemy and the avenger."

Psalm 8:2

"Jesus saith unto them, Yea; have ye never read, Out of the mouth of babes and sucklings thou hast perfected praise?"

Matthew 21:16

God has ordained praise. In the mouth of a believer, praise can stop Satan in his tracks.

CD SIX
The Power of Praise

"I will be glad and rejoice
in thee: I will sing praise to
thy name, O thou most High.
When mine enemies are turned
back, they shall fall
and perish at thy presence."
Psalm 9:2-3

God Himself inhabits our praises.

Praise Brings the Very Presence and Power of God on the Scene

FOCUS: "But thou art holy, O thou that inhabitest the praises of Israel" (Psalm 22:3).

Why should we praise God? Psalm 8:1-2 tells us, "O Lord our Lord, how excellent is thy name in all the earth! who hast set thy glory above the heavens. Out of the mouth of babes and sucklings hast thou ordained strength because of thine enemies, that thou mightest still the enemy and the avenger." Matthew 21:16 says it this way: "Yea; have ye never read, Out of the mouth of babes and sucklings thou hast perfected praise?" Jesus uses the words *strength* and *praise* interchangeably. There is strength or power in praise. That's why God has ordained it. Praise stops Satan.

> *Praise brings the very presence and power of God on the scene.*

Psalm 9:2-3 says, "I will be glad and rejoice in thee: I will sing praise to thy name, O thou most High. When mine enemies are turned back, they shall fall and perish at thy presence." This says *when* your enemies are turned back and fall, not *if* they do. That is a promise. When you begin to praise God, your enemies will be stopped.

Jesus won the battle over your enemy, Satan. As you enforce his defeat, you enforce your own victory. Remind the devil of Calvary. Offer a sacrifice of praise to God continually for your victory over him (Hebrews 13:15). Psalm 9:1 in *The Amplified*

Bible says, "I will praise You, O Lord, with my whole heart; I will show forth (recount and tell aloud) all Your marvelous works and wonderful deeds!" When you do that, the enemy can't stand it and is ready to leave. James 4:7 says, "Submit yourselves therefore to God. Resist the devil, and he will flee from you." Praise offers resistance to the enemy.

> *When you praise God, your enemies will be stopped.*

You cast him out. *You* still the avenger. *You* put on the shield of faith. Do not wait for God to do it for you. Through Jesus, God has done all He is ever going to do, and Jesus did a complete work.

So don't ask God to deal with the enemy for you. The Apostle Paul tried that and it didn't work.

Because Paul had received an abundance of revelation knowledge, Satan sent one of his messengers to afflict and persecute him in order to steal the Word that was sown in Paul's heart (2 Corinthians 12:7). God had taught him truths like "Put on the whole armour of God, that ye may be able to stand against the wiles of the devil" (Ephesians 6:11). Paul knew the Word. But like many Christians today, he wasn't doing what he knew to do.

Instead, Paul turned to God to get the devil off him. But God said, "My grace is sufficient for thee" (2 Corinthians 12:9). In other words, God was saying to Paul, "You are equipped with My strength and My very presence in your inner man so that you can overcome the devil or any circumstance that comes your way. Therefore, *you* take the authority you have in Christ, resist the devil and he will flee from you." That's good advice for us today!

If Satan is operating with any proficiency in the affairs of your life, here are some checkpoints to consider: (1) If there is any sin in your life, confess it and receive your forgiveness. (2) Check the amount of time you are spending in the Word. (3) Check the amount of time spent in prayer, fellowshiping with the Father. (4) Is the praise of God going forth from your lips?

God inhabits the praises of His people (Psalm 22:3). He is present in praise. That is why praise has power against the enemy. No matter how foolish it may seem, it gets results.

All Judah and the inhabitants of Jerusalem proved it works when their enemies came against them. The Spirit of God told them, "The battle is not yours, but God's" (2 Chronicles 20:15).

> And when he [Jehoshaphat] had consulted with the people, he appointed singers unto the Lord, and that should praise the beauty of holiness, as they went out before the army, and to say, Praise the Lord; for his mercy endureth for ever. And when they began to sing and to praise, the Lord set ambushments against the children of Ammon, Moab, and mount Seir, which were come against Judah; and they were smitten. For the children of Ammon and Moab stood up against the inhabitants of mount Seir, utterly to slay and destroy them: and when they had made an end of the inhabitants of Seir, every one helped to destroy another (verses 21-23).

Praise brought God on the scene and the battle was won! The same can happen in your life.

Now Begin Enjoying It

Out of the abundance of the heart the mouth speaks (Matthew 12:34; Luke 6:45). When you have a praise in your heart, it will come out your mouth. You'll get a praise in your heart when you begin to put the Word in there. So look for all the good things God has done and begin to talk about them.

The Word says we should offer the sacrifice of praise to God continually. No matter how we feel, as we praise Him, He will instantly be on the scene. His presence and power are ready to give you the victory!

$\mathcal{CD}$ 6 $Outlined$

I. Praise is strength (power), which stills the enemy and the avenger (Psalm 8:2; Matthew 21:16; Psalm 9:2-3)

II. Jesus won the battle but the victory is yours
   A. God did through Jesus all He is going to do
   B. It is up to *you*, not God, to resist the devil (James 4:7; Psalm 9:1)

III. The Apostle Paul wanted God to get the devil off him (2 Corinthians 12:7-8)
   A. God's grace was sufficient to do the job (2 Corinthians 12:9)
   B. Paul already had, in Christ, the authority to stop the enemy

IV. Here are some checkpoints to consider if Satan is operating with any proficiency in your life
   A. If there is sin in your life, confess it and receive forgiveness
   B. How much time are you spending in the Word?
   C. How much time are you spending in prayer, fellowshiping with the Father?
   D. Is the praise of God going forth from your lips?

V. God inhabits praise (Psalm 22:3)
   A. Praise brings the presence and power of God on the scene
   B. Judah and the inhabitants of Jerusalem sang and praised the Lord and their enemies destroyed each other (2 Chronicles 20:21-23)

Study Questions

(1) Why should we praise God? _____
_____
_____
_____

(2) Jesus won the battle over Satan, but what can we do to walk in that
victory? _____
_____
_____
_____

(3) Explain what God meant when He told the Apostle Paul, "My grace
is sufficient for thee." _____
_____
_____
_____

(4) List the checkpoints to consider if Satan is working with any proficiency in your life. _____
_____
_____
_____

(5) What did Jehoshaphat have the people do when their enemies came
against them? _____
_____
_____
_____

Study Notes

"A good man out of the good treasure of his heart
bringeth forth that which is good...."
Luke 6:45

Prayer for Salvation and Baptism in the Holy Spirit

Heavenly Father, I come to You in the Name of Jesus. Your Word says, "Whosoever shall call on the name of the Lord shall be saved" (Acts 2:21). I am calling on You. I pray and ask Jesus to come into my heart and be Lord over my life according to Romans 10:9-10: "If thou shalt confess with thy mouth the Lord Jesus, and shalt believe in thine heart that God hath raised him from the dead, thou shalt be saved. For with the heart man believeth unto righteousness; and with the mouth confession is made unto salvation." I do that now. I confess that Jesus is Lord, and I believe in my heart that God raised Him from the dead. I repent of sin. I renounce it. I renounce the devil and everything he stands for. Jesus is my Lord.

I am now reborn! I am a Christian—a child of Almighty God! I am saved! You also said in Your Word, "If ye then, being evil, know how to give good gifts unto your children: HOW MUCH MORE shall your heavenly Father give the Holy Spirit to them that ask him?" (Luke 11:13). I'm also asking You to fill me with the Holy Spirit. Holy Spirit, rise up within me as I praise God. I fully expect to speak with other tongues as You give me the utterance (Acts 2:4). In Jesus' Name. Amen!

Begin to praise God for filling you with the Holy Spirit. Speak those words and syllables you receive—not in your own language, but the language given to you by the Holy Spirit. You have to use your own voice. God will not force you to speak. Don't be concerned with how it sounds. It is a heavenly language!

Continue with the blessing God has given you and pray in the spirit every day.

You are a born-again, Spirit-filled believer. You'll never be the same!

Find a good church that boldly preaches God's Word and obeys it. Become part of a church family who will love and care for you as you love and care for them.

We need to be connected to each other. It increases our strength in God. It's God's plan for us.

Make it a habit to watch the Believer's Voice of Victory Network and become a doer of the Word, who is blessed in his doing (James 1:22-25).

About the Author

Kenneth Copeland is co-founder and president of Kenneth Copeland Ministries in Fort Worth, Texas, and best-selling author of books that include *Honor—Walking in Honesty, Truth and Integrity,* and *THE BLESSING of The LORD Makes Rich and He Adds No Sorrow With It.*

Since 1967, Kenneth has been a minister of the gospel of Christ and teacher of God's Word. He is also the artist on award-winning albums such as his Grammy-nominated *Only the Redeemed, In His Presence, He Is Jehovah, Just a Closer Walk* and *Big Band Gospel.* He also co-stars as the character Wichita Slim in the children's adventure videos *The Gunslinger, Covenant Rider* and the movie *The Treasure of Eagle Mountain,* and as Daniel Lyon in the Commander Kellie and the Superkids™ videos *Armor of Light* and *Judgment: The Trial of Commander Kellie.* Kenneth also co-stars as a Hispanic godfather in the 2009 and 2016 movies *The Rally* and *The Rally 2: Breaking the Curse.*

With the help of offices and staff in the United States, Canada, England, Australia, South Africa and Ukraine, Kenneth is fulfilling his vision to boldly preach the uncompromised WORD of God from the top of this world, to the bottom, and all the way around. His ministry reaches millions of people worldwide through daily and Sunday TV broadcasts, magazines, teaching audios and videos, conventions and campaigns, and the World Wide Web.

When The LORD first spoke to Kenneth and Gloria Copeland about starting the *Believer's Voice of Victory* magazine...

He said: *This is your seed. Give it to everyone who ever responds to your ministry, and don't ever allow anyone to pay for a subscription!*

For more than 50 years, it has been the joy of Kenneth Copeland Ministries to bring the good news to believers. Readers enjoy teaching from ministers who write from lives of living contact with God, and testimonies from believers experiencing victory through God's WORD in their everyday lives.

Today, the *BVOV* magazine is mailed monthly, bringing encouragement and blessing to believers around the world. Many even use it as a ministry tool, passing it on to others who desire to know Jesus and grow in their faith!

Request your FREE subscription to the *Believer's Voice of Victory* magazine today!

Go to **freevictory.com** to subscribe online, or call us at
1-800-600-7395 (U.S. only) or **+1-817-852-6000**.

We're Here for You!®

Your growth in God's WORD and victory in Jesus are at the very center of our hearts. In every way God has equipped us, we will help you deal with the issues facing you, so you can be the **victorious overcomer** He has planned for you to be.

The mission of Kenneth Copeland Ministries is about all of us growing and going together. Our prayer is that you will take full advantage of all The LORD has given us to share with you.

Wherever you are in the world, you can watch the *Believer's Voice of Victory* broadcast on television (check your local listings), the Internet at kcm.org or on our digital Roku channel.

Our website, **kcm.org,** gives you access to every resource we've developed for your victory. And, you can find contact information for our international offices in Africa, Australia, Canada, Europe, Ukraine and our headquarters in the United States.

Each office is staffed with devoted men and women, ready to serve and pray with you. You can contact the worldwide office nearest you for assistance, and you can call us for prayer at our U.S. number, 1-817-852-6000, seven days a week!

We encourage you to connect with us often and let us be part of your everyday walk of faith!

Jesus Is LORD!

Kenneth & Gloria Copeland

Kenneth and Gloria Copeland